The revelation that the Father gives about His Son Jesus to show us the things that will take place soon…

Written by: Paola Ruth Aramayo M.
Illustrated by: Mariana Ferreira

Copyright © 2025 Paola Ruth Aramayo M.
Illustrations © 2025 Mariana Ferreira
All rights reserved.

No part of this publication may be reproduced, stored in a retrieval system, or transmitted in any form or by any means—electronic, mechanical, photocopying, recording, or otherwise—without prior written permission from the author and illustrator, except for brief quotations in reviews or academic references.

This book is a creative teaching resource inspired by the Book of Revelation. While it does not directly quote scripture, it seeks to convey biblical themes in a way that is engaging and accessible for children.

All illustrations and text are the intellectual property of the author and illustrator and may not be used without written consent.

ISBN: 978-1-953199-09-6
Printed in the U.S.A.

For more information, visit www.pinpoint.pub

Hi, how are you? My name is Talita.
Have you heard about a King who will come from a place
called PARADISE to rule with justice over
the earth for all eternity? *Luke 23:43*

The King's name is Jesus. He lived on the earth, but a dragon wanted
to take His place and make many people go far away from
King Jesus and forget about Him.

So, the Father of King Jesus took Him to live in PARADISE to prepare and wait for the time when He could return and take back His Kingdom.

King Jesus is waiting for the people to think about Him and repent of their bad ways and abandon the dragon.

When that happens, He will return and remain on the earth to rule FOREVER! There is so much more to know about King Jesus.

The Father of King Jesus gave Him special powers to destroy the dragon.

There are seven very important letters that King Jesus sent us before He returns. Would you like to read them with me?

Hi. **Don't lose the love in your heart.** If you take care of it, I will give you a very special tree that bears fruit that never rots and when you eat the fruit you will have eternal life.

Yours truly, King Jesus

#1

How are you? I want to encourage you to defeat evil. **If you are full of love, there will be no place in your heart for fear.** If you defeat fear, I will give you the crown of life. It will be so precious.

With love, King Jesus

#2

What's up? There is something very important that you should avoid because it can really hurt you. **You must defeat lies and not let deception enter your heart.** If you always tell the truth, I will give you a very special food. Delicious! I will also give you a new name and I will write your new name on a beautiful white stone.

Take care, King Jesus

#3

Hello. I want to remind you how important it is to **not have bad thoughts or bad desires in your heart.** If you can do it, I will give you so much authority and power so that you can rule the nations with Me.

See you soon, King Jesus

#4

Hi there! I desire, with all My heart, that you pay close attention to what you do. There are some things that make you get mad and that's not good. **Everything that you do, do it with joy and love.** If you do, I will give you some beautiful clothes as a gift, just like Mine. I also have a Book of Life where I will write your name and never erase it.

Hugs, King Jesus

#5

I am so happy to send you this letter so that you can put into practice all that I am asking you to do. **When things get difficult, don't forget that I will protect you.** Remember, I will always take care of you, even in hard times. Just don't forget about these letters that I wrote to you, and you will be able to live with Me in my Father's beautiful house.

With love, King Jesus

#6

Here I am sending you My last letter: **Don't let pride control your heart.** Don't treat others badly. I have a humble heart, so try to be like Me.
If your heart is calm and humble, you can sit on a throne beside Me.

#7 See you real soon, King Jesus

Do you know where King Jesus was when He sent these letters to us?
Well, He sent them from a place called PARADISE and we are going to find out everything we can about this interesting place.

How exciting! There is a great throne where the Father of King Jesus is seated.
Around the throne there is an emerald rainbow.

Also, by His side, there are four angels each with six wings.

There are twenty-four elders with crowns, dressed in white sitting on thrones and along with the angels they sing:
HOLY, HOLY, HOLY.

Before the throne there are seven lamps of fire and
there is a sea of crystal glass. Wow! How amazing! *Revelation 4:1-11*

While we see all this Heavenly beauty in PARADISE,
on the earth the dragon and his army want to force the people
to worship and obey him.

The dragon wants to be the King and he causes lots of pain for
those who don't accept him.

That is why the Father told King Jesus: Son, it's time to return to earth, I will give you a **scroll that is closed with seven seals that only You can open** and a battle plan to weaken the dragon and his kingdom of darkness.

So, King Jesus took the scroll in His hands and opened the seals. Do you want to know what happened next? Let's find out. *Revelation 5*

When King Jesus opens **the first four seals**, four warriors appear on four different horses to weaken the dragon.

The first horse is White, the second horse is Red, the third horse is Black, and the fourth horse is Yellow.

When King Jesus opens the **FIFTH SEAL** there is an earthquake on the earth and the sun gets dark and the moon turns red.

Then, Jesus opens the **SIXTH SEAL** and His Father puts a seal of **PROTECTION** over everyone who read and obeyed in their heart the words written in the seven letters of King Jesus.

But when King Jesus opens the SEVENTH SEAL, seven angels with seven trumpets appear and get ready to play them. *Revelation 8*

The first, second, third, fourth, fifth and sixth trumpets sound. When **the seventh trumpet sounds, it's the signal that it is now time for King Jesus to come** to earth.

King Jesus appears in the clouds and **everyone who has the Father's SEAL OF PROTECTION** begins to **fly towards Him** to gather together in the clouds.

Then, their bodies are transformed in the clouds, and they have superpowers like King Jesus to come down to earth and rule with Him.

Revelation 19:11
1 Thessalonians 4:17

As part of the battle plan that the Father gave to King Jesus, another seven angels come and pour out seven bowls filled with punishment for the dragon and his evil army.

Then the dragon and his army are cast into prison for a thousand years until the **day of the final judgment.**

Then Jesus arrives to His Royal City called BEULAH and from there, He begins to rule over all the earth. *Isaiah 62:4*

HALLELUJAH!
HALLELUJAH!
HALLELUJAH!

There is joy in PARADISE and on the earth and everyone begins to say: Our King Jesus is Powerful and He reigns! Salvation, honor, glory and power to our King Jesus. Hallelujah!

Now everything begins to change. King Jesus brings restoration to all the earth. Children will live for many many years! People begin to enjoy all the work of their hands. The rivers are purified, they are no longer dirty.

The wolf and the lamb eat together.

The lion no longer eats meat, it eats grass like the ox.

The serpent only eats dirt, it no longer bites. *Isaiah 65:17-25*

I am so happy! There is so much joy in my heart to see that there will be no more evil on the earth.

King Jesus is preparing the earth to receive His Father who will also come down from PARADISE with His Heavenly Throne.

When the Father of King Jesus sees that all the earth is prepared and restored, then He will release the dragon and all of his army from the prison to destroy them forever and from that moment on, there will be no more death. *Revelation 21*

The Father will feel so much love and happiness in His heart that He will bring His home down from PARADISE. It is so big and beautiful. The doors are pearls! The entire floor is gold, the walls are full of precious stones.

Inside the house there is a GARDEN, it is so beautiful because it has a crystal-clear river. In the middle there is a special tree that produces twelve fruits all the time, the leaves of the tree are medicine.

There will be no more sickness, pain, or sadness.

There are many other marvelous things to see inside the Kingdom of King Jesus and His Father. Would you like to live there?
Let's go! There is a place for everyone!

Would you like to pray with me?

Jesus, I want you to be my King. I want you to come
and rule and restore the whole earth.

Clean my hands and my heart of anything evil so that
I can rule with You.

Thank you for loving me and protecting me.
Thank you because you want to change my sadness to joy,
help me to guard and obey Your words.

AMEN.

(THERE IS NO)

ACKNOWLEDGMENTS

First, I want to thank God, the Holy Spirit, and my King and Savior Jesus for placing in me the desire and ability to write this book.

I am thankful for my loving husband Curtis for all the support he gave me and for enjoying each page with me. For motivating me to keep pressing on and making this book a reality.

I am thankful for MiSion (Center for Ministry Training) in Argentina, which holds a special place in my heart and for each teacher for helping me understand God's Plan for the End Times.

I am thankful for my friend and sister in Christ, Mariana Ferreira, for giving shape and color to the illustrations that the Lord showed me in dreams and visions.

Contact info for the author

www.ingramcontent.com/pod-product-compliance
Lightning Source LLC
Chambersburg PA
CBHW061349010526
44107CB00011B/884